FUTURE SYMPTOMS

Also by A. Molotkov:

The Catalog of Broken Things
Application of Shadows
Synonyms for Silence

Future Symptoms

A. Molotkov

THE WORD WORKS
WASHINGTON, D. C.

THE WORD WORKS
P.O. Box 42164
Washington, D.C. 20015
editor@wordworksbooks.org

Cover art: A. Molotkov
Cover: Susan Pearce Design
Interior Design: Kirby Vaillant-White
Author photograph: Laura Stahman

ISBN: 978-1-944585-51-8
LCCN: 2022931864

Acknowledgments

The Antioch Review: "Ten Mysteries"
Arts & Letters: "Prayer to a Future Self," "Endless Happy Returns,"
    "The Other Side of a Photograph"
Asheville Poetry Review: "Self-Portrait" (1)
Atlanta Review: "Ten Love Stories"
Bedouin Books: "To Paul Celan"
Bennington Review: "René Magritte"
Boone's Dock Press: "Hunger for Information" (published as part of
    the chapbook *True Stories from the Future*)
The Brooklyn Review: "Ten Theories"
The Cincinnati Review: "Ten Tools"
Cider Press Review: "Self-Portrait" (2)
Coal Hill Review: "Testaments from the Departed"
DMQ Review: "Ten Doors"
Event: "Heart Problems"
Ghost Town Poetry Anthology: "The engineer of my dreams"
Hotel Amerika: "The Static Lives of Nightingales"
January Review: "Final Report," "Ghostliness"
Mantis: "The Small Bang"
Midwest Quarterly: "Afteretiquette," "Blood Exercise," "First"
Naugatuck River Review: "Aperture"
Nixes Mate Review: "Round Trip"
North Dakota Review: "Prayer"
One: "Unpunctuation"
Prairie Schooner: "A Study in Luminosity," "The Melting Star"
RHINO Poetry: "Complicit in Incompleteness"
Roanoke Review: "Bridging the Memory"
Salamander: "Optimism," "Breath's Opinion," "Obituary"
Saint Ann's Review: "Ways Around It"
Sisyphus: "The Sum of Your Life," "Appointment with Inner Self"
Takoma Literary Review: "The time before"
Toe Good Poetry: "Ten Questions" (also published as part of the
    chapbook *The Invention of Distance*)
Twenty20: "History Lesson"

Wikimedia: "Solar Wind," winner of the 2019 Heart of
        Knowledge contest
The Worchester Review: "Unlove"
Zone 3: "Ten Tens"

Found language in "Solar Wind": excerpts from my father's
article in *The Astrophysical Journal,* 859:39 (5pp), 2018 May 20
(I.A. Molotkov, B. Atamaniuk, "An Analysis of Processes in the
Solar Wind in a Thin Layer Adjacent to the Front of the Shock
Wave").

My most sincere gratitude to the members of The Moonlit
Poetry Caravan for their help with revisions: Frances Payne
Adler, Jon Boisvert, Erica Braverman, Diane Corson, Willa
Schneberg, Sam Seskin, Jeff Whitney, John Sibley Williams.

Special thanks to Laurie for her support and for the inspiration.

❧

Contents

Air Wisdoms

100

I keep my hands small
to touch the world lightly
as it wants to be touched

The Melting Star

That grimace, the way you bite
your lower lip. The pain
is back. Any day, we'll

pack a suitcase. I remember
the dew by our tent as we

camped and the way snow
fell in all directions and
life was too

bright to live. The world,
described in so many

ways, fit its shifting
meaning. You caught
a snowflake in your

palm. *Look
here, a star.*

Minus Air

Isn't this a beautiful
world with virus and human
beings? I can't

breathe,

but where is
breath among the many
things constrained?

I was I was not I was here, thinking, breathing, not breathing

I'm George
Floyd I'm not George
Floyd

I'm in this quarantine section, and they
won't let my
mother in my brother my
sister in husband in
I will draw
draw

my

last

breath

> *without them*

> *the child draws a face, two*
> *eyes and a*
> *mask*

with each exhale
our lungs reject

the air they sought
and seek again
what's not

theirs

> *I'm George*
> *Floyd I'm not George*
> *Floyd*

Look how steady the mirror
where breath
was

> lying

water, frozen

How

long
can you feed these

buzzing machines?

I
miss you

Unventilator

You replace yourself with an empty space
How does it feel?
An extreme subtraction? A sta-
tistic?

I was worried about the increased
risk among minorities

(as if)

The more
die the
less every
1
matters?

They

matter

(as if my
concerns concern
the ~~President~~)

What's the
~~President~~
made
of?

I'm George
Floyd I'm not George
Floyd

Imagine all the dead, singing

Consider those you love going about
their daily tasks without you

Life, a sum that swallows its parts,
happy with your silence

Face mask, as if
there were another
kind

I was thinking of the
space around
breath absorbing
breath

as if police
brutality
were not
enough

Diagnosis

the edge
            of body

incision
            from inside
        without scalpel's
sharp
eyesight
lungs full of tears
at the end
of what
is
            named, breathed
in
            our bleeding
language

one ventilator
two ventilators
three

I'm George
Floyd I'm not George
Floyd

Undiagnosis

The corona crowns the
~~President~~

Imagine the dead,
returning

fighting for
air

The virus pretends
to be
your own
body

Premonition

Red fever, and
these red
thoughts

                    I

breathe loss into light,
trip on life's red syllables
as their rhythm breaks me

Air is not enough

Not
        enough air is not enough

               My own
               body killed me

                        Some of me is in your lungs

              Not every

               reason

            to die is a good
              reason

Obligation?

Friends of the deceased dodge
questions of substance, pounce
on anecdotes, compare

vital signs I saw

                                    you

through thick
glass, so thin I knew time
had
broken

                                    you

in half

your ashes in the urn
invulnerable, a hole

in the world where
you were

                    Imagine all the dead, speaking

You As Me or So

You open your eyes,
your face gray like the pillow

                                        Is there
                                    ever a way to

                                        return?

                                        Do birds
                                    return? Do
                                        fish?

                            The ~~President~~ claimed
                                    all credit

When spring comes back, it's not
the same spring

Your life,
a mirror, reflecting
someplace else, as if this
moment were
different
from the next
this generation
different than

this person's

suffering

Face your face
You are George
Floyd you are not George
Floyd

How steady the mirror
where you
were

Language Acquisition

We've found
                    words

for explaining
our inaction

Our ~~hearts~~
were

closed, then gone—a curious

glitch of anatomy

                    The ~~President~~
                        is
                    the virus

                                        Each
                of us spins on an axis of self, inscrutable,
                on a shorter or longer orbit, marginally

                                        stable

We don't mean to be
selfish, to focus so
obsessively on our

                    small problems

Time bends around us, blurs

others out of focus
with tears

The ~~President~~
contributes
tear gas

Diagnosis

I am Eric
Garner I am not
Eric Garner My

ghost wakes me up, worried
"What's wrong?" I ask

                                        It's the rustle
                                    of last year's leaves
                                    I can't get out of my
                                                    mind

                                            It's the same

                                                    thing

                                    happening again to
                                        George Floyd

                        Human beings
                        without air
                            piles
                        of protein

As if the virus were not
enough numbers
adding
up to a

~~President~~

I'm the
~~President~~ I'm not
the ~~President~~ I
didn't vote for
the ~~President~~
my
~~parents~~ voted
for the
~~President~~
I didn't
vote for my
parents

wake
up
someone who can
fix this

they
were
killed by
the ~~Pre=~~
~~sident~~
what's the
~~President~~
made of,
Ameri
ca?

Sometimes air is enough

Breath, and
the space around
breath where
the knee is

we must be a missing
infinity when
we die

I open
windows invite
fresh air

where the knee is

you could
hardly breathe in the dim
light

you

beautiful
volcano nowhere on this
planet

*Am I your face
mask?*

Poli(ce)tics

~~Ask me a question, any question~~ *I want to hold on to you Just because you died, don't say it's impossible Out the window, the poplar* ~~remembers~~ *through the glass*

Was this before or after?

I'm George
Floyd I'm not George
Floyd

I was worried about
mortality rate more
than my own
mortality

The virus
pretends
to be
the ~~President~~

The monstrous sea inside
your lungs, your body's

slow

descent
Act now, feel night's fingertips

(as if)

Look how steady
the mirror

You'd see
your
face if your
eyes could still
see

As if none of your messages
were ever delivered

The President praised himself I'm not
responsible for the
President?

I'm
innocent?

Cold like love, breath escapes

Let
loose

The virus does
not
discriminate
without the help
from the President

The ~~President~~
contributes
tear
gas to
help
with breathing

Listen to your last thought with water's edge inside your
lungs, creeping
water line, life
            long crossed and song
                    forgotten

Your lungs don't

mind

No mystery in this
end of being

The ~~President~~, made
of something
much worse
:
sixty-two
million
little
~~presidents~~

Theories for Endings

A knee
on your neck, virus
in your lungs

Sixty-two million
knees

Wait
wait,
George
Floyd

linger with

me

longer

(as if)

there's

always a reason
to go,
but

not
this

linger and tell
your tale

not this
unreason

Entropy Lessons

Complicit in Incompleteness

I'm moved by how   the world
moves past me, grows   its new
shapes, its   myriad threads. I long
to disappear inside   myself—my
door   so worn only the frame
holds it in place.   The moment
—and then,   its other side, its
under-   pinnings before and
after us. How   to imagine
completely, without   being inside
the imagined? An empty   bed.
A narrow path   from heart to
mouth to   a scolding blue sky.
Broken   glass where skin
might be. I'm moved   by how
the world moves me. How   to
love more completely   given
another chance,   this one?

Unlove

if I lived on the surface of the sun I
would burn for the rest of my life
without going to hell like a moth I
would miss you I miss you anyway I
crawl through you like a broken mir-
ror I cry from your eyes when I'm free
I stand before you bleeding if I lived
on the surface of the sun I would miss
you

Ways Around It

Life as an accident,   a fire, an
explosion,   ~~future~~ added and
subtracted   as we curve careful-
ly around   our intended paths,
rubbing   our mistakes off on
those   who love us. In   the
cellars of our minds lie   full
chests of love and gold, but   we
don't know which is   love and
which is gold   and which,
last week's   lunch or a ~~memory~~
from many   years ago, an anchor
in the dark. The fireworks   and
their reflections   in your eyes and
how   you said, *I can't do   this
anymore*—how could   you, in
this expiring   ~~future~~, with these
effortless lights, your   lungs full
of holes.

The Other Side of a Photograph

With the tip of my tongue, I touch
your   eyebrows.   Silhouettes
move under the eyelids. The road
in autumn: dry leaves,   shady
passages, narrow green   rows.
Who knows another enough   to
be   certain?   Who   can   say
everything before silence? As I
walk out from under the crown   of
a pine tree, is our future   already
set for us? Dry   leaves, shady
passages. Who's   to say there
is anything   permanent? What
is that expression   on your
face?

Prayer to a ~~Future~~ Self

A garden of arrows grows from
my skin.   You love like sand,
remember   like   water,   drift
through   me   unexplored,   like
indifference.   You may be a
phantom, but I believe in you: your
memory is accurate and helpful.
Brief,   we shape the world before
we crash, unfit for replay. How   to
tell love from unlove: the moon,
the blood,   the silence. I read the
steam of your breath, am your
silhouette, travel in your thoughts.
When   you are free, translate me
into your language. Learn   me
by heart, as a song learns its singer.
Erase me.

Endless Happy Returns

a blue crane descending from the sky
invites me to fly to cure my pains *silly*
I reply *there is no difference between be-
ing trapped on the ground and in a crane
flock* white acacias stretch thorny arms
begging me to stay *don't cry my death
is only an attempt to return* I ask an
orange alligator about life *it's a chase
after those who leave or an attempt to
escape*

Skin's Commitment

I take a fast boat down your blood
stream to see what you're about because
I want to love you when I return I will
hold your hand for months ask new
questions seep through cracks in your
skin where you need me

Self-Portrait

This *I*, a tweaked   angel turned
inside out, soul   of plastic, white
dust, white   memory. The past
is   powder. Objects bleed
molecules, fill my   wheelbarrow
with questions, not   all belonging
to me. How   do I fit everything
finite,   everything entranced,
like   the world itself: its   face,
its shivering body, its   pink dawn,
its   long white day, its   bright,
masterful night? It's   not   my
stop, but I   step out, not my
life but I   make it mine.

History Lesson

One day a city was   built, then it
was   destroyed. Somewhere
in between passed   our lives,
long   like an eyelash.

Heart Problems

In the corner of my heart lives a small
bird without a passport. It sings, but
not for me. Dimly, the day accepts me.
I shiver in its excessive promise. When
a flower fades, is it disqualified? Let
me lie attached to my gravity center,
pulling, pulling away. Does a mute
song capture hearts? I would arrange
a forest in my heart, sing high up on
a branch, but the bird scowls at me,
turns my song to silence.

The engineer of my dreams

leaves work early   has other
things to do   other minds to stir
for the rest of the night my dreams are
unattended   unreliable   they
don't follow the rules   like a
drunken sailor overnight in an
imaginary port

Aperture

I scream and wake and scream and
wake and you wake and scream. We
are like this. Driving too fast to tell—a
cemetery on the left, an orchard on the
right. Let me tell you the story of how
it all began before it ended. I scream,
and you scream, and the driver in the
opposite lane screams and the brakes
screech. I've been here. Apple trees.
We are like this when we break open
too soon. Let me think of it my way:
the center of gravity pulling us in. The
moment before, already knowing.

Body Facts

Prayer

Rewind my brain, reprogram
my life to your own style. Reset

my dead neurons. I wait,

digital like a newborn child,
a universe of bits

at my fingertips. I was born

to this story I didn't write. If you
want honesty, take my blood

test, an MRI. For urgency,

write me into a crime story,
make me the crime. Arrest me

microscopically. I want to

live in you, breathe
your 3D mystery.

The time before

the sheets are cold, before

the warmth escapes them. Moments
splattered in yolk, their boiled
inner sanctums reduced to protein, skeletons

hanging on the thread of time whose tight
curve will not hold us. The snow
ascends – and as we watch, the slow

crack-and-hiss of a stuck record player, from my past.

*

A shortcut through the woods. A slanted

sun through my skin slices life into now
and not, the shadow of many years until
I write this, as I emerge, a blond child, headed

to the beach, learning to disappear.

*

These strings I pull through me, as if they were

the song, dawn's junky veins before
and after us. We spread
our love over this spare land, let it grow inside

our bodies. We dissipate along the thread, our names
handles on doors forever nailed shut, our hopes
abandoned among the world's

small claims. At least there is a thread, a little time
to look for it, the time before warmth
escapes, before the body

is cold.

Self-portrait

Morning
star, can you
hold as I cross

the river and the sky

wraps me softly? Dew
or tears – no one
can tell. The body's

secret: it is

the whole
of me after all. I'm
barely here. Morning

star, shine on

my absence. Short
death with its long
victory song.

Mission of Empathy

The Other is the poor and destitute one, and nothing which
concerns this Stranger can leave the I indifferent.
—Emmanuel Levinas

Laughing stranger, how
      can you face so
            beautifully this
hesitant world? Surely the wind
      is at your fingertips, future
            warming up to you. How
can I know you best?

Dying stranger, alone
      in your cell, face
            furrowed by worry and dust. Your
shaking hands. Light bulb
      on a wire; every
            dark thing you shared. How
did you weave your perilous days?

Tired stranger, an intersecting line
      in living geometry. Here we are. Every
            string was pulled so
we could meet. Your face
      shines with mysteries
            to learn. How
can I hear you clearly?

Unpunctuation

If you need a new spelling
for your question mark, use my body

to wash away your mistakes. I open
into a landscape. A few hills,

a few cows, the river's shining line
under the red light from my arteries. My blood

feeds the river, but we don't
talk about it. We follow it

to the cloudy ocean inside my skull's
cavity. It's half-full. It has

many islands: love, panic,
mystery. On each island, you

and I discuss river endings. I
open up into a flood. A few

waves, a few boats, the blue light
from my veins, half-empty. If you need

a longer period for your
question mark, hold me back

with your
small fingers.

Optimism

Butterfly feast, hillside
on fire. So many

bright things dulled

in the wind. This is how
we pass, unnoticed.

Testaments from the Departed

I prefer a body
        to its
           absence.
Simple things
              last under fire:
a needle, a knife,
        a skeleton,

              street without
end, crumbling
        red brick of these
            cemetery walls. In the end,

there is no
        end that we know of, just
            a concept. I'll
see you some-
        where.

***

Translate me
        into clay
            into words
into light. Enable
            lasting.
Restore hunger to
        my lips.
                All those
        unsaid things—
a garden
        of lost
            thoughts—

give them
          meaning.
                    Translate me
                              into yourself.

***

On the bottom
               shelf,
my shadow.

The middle,
               a mirror
holds my face.

On the top
               a jar
with my
               ashes.
Room

               full

of air.

The Small Bang

I wrote a recipe
        for keeping death away
                        in shorthand,
the hour hand,

but when the hour passed,
        the next was identical in its place,
my recipe remained
        applicable

and unnecessary just as we are,
        so determined to stay
                and incapable of staying,
                        like all things,

turning into their opposites
        as we turn into not-us
                as a full glass turns empty
if I wait long enough,

        like the big bang,
                so short,
                        so full of future.

Final Report

It's safer with a heart in bubble wrap. Do I
still have a license? This rusty

handle opens my head. Forgive me: I haven't
had a chance to clean up. Would you

hold my skeleton's hand? I don't have all
my bones to show at the checkpoint. I falsified

my fingers and my fingertips. I made
omissions on my entry form. I forgot

to say I love you.

Breath's Opinion

in memory of Sam Seskin

All I know is: at this
moment, a young scholar solves

a century-old problem. A group of six
climbs Everest, a group of twelve

is rescued from a hurricane. The same
smile faces us in the mirror after

all these years, but we are
so much smarter, so

lovingly open. And just now,
the doctor is born who will

cure everything that ails us, in
other patients. Easy now, don't

be sad, small engine. There is too much
breathing left to do.

Ghostliness

Is your body corporeal or
remembered? You left a silence,
an apple core, me in the corner, staring

at a spiderweb. You hung
a light ray across the river

valley beneath the mountain, then
removed the river. What
do you say to those who still

have hope? What about a heart
on a wire, a brain with cutouts? Literal

wire, literal things I won't mention. I
dive under an iceberg, deeper,
deeper, waiting for it

to begin.

The Static Lives of Nightingales

I wish I were a long
distance bus driver

propelling a warm
bus along the world's

highways. But I'm only
a nightingale salesman

whose birds perch
obediently for display

chirping their
predictable melody

if only I could
drive that bus

forever without a stop
without looking back

along the highway

Unchronology

If the bridge explodes, the river
grows a new one. Our lost

limbs, lost memories return. Time
is drawn out of us by the hook

of each breath. I love faces
of strangers opening to their lives. In

the gaps between memories, lie
opportunities we missed. Days

stack on the sharp axis of being. Time
draws on us in wrinkles the way

moments align along a string
that doesn't exist.

Air Wisdoms

Instruments of Perspective

I hide inside those I love, without
letting them know. Why

pressure them? They weave
the long paths of their lives

amidst minefields. They might
find me if they wish. And to

those who visit: if you
bring the right key, you may

open me. Inside, a new set
of sheets, an hourglass,

a compass, a tuning fork.
On the third shelf, a mirror

with your own face, its
beauty you question, but I

so easily see.

Solar Wind

as we face each
other with our
well-built smiles

in a thin layer
of the shock wave

the world another
gigantic
mirror staring back

the temperature is
added to the list
of unknown quantities

magnetic reconnection
the merging
of magnetic islands

we may experience

this dead silence between
us this harsh
grimace

are potential traps letting
through

symptoms of
our desperate lifelong
asking

locally
accelerated particles

for our inner quick
burning

the magnitude
of induction decreases

but would it be enough
if we weren't

flares with unusual power

emmeshed in light all
along

in the solar wind

trying to love
ourselves out of this

Obituary

I welcome emptiness. It is
        a good start. An empty
                vessel holds no dynamite. An empty

mind plans no atrocities. Hold
        my hand and share
                how it feels, to plan

your own exit. I respect
        every part of it. I love
                the empty frame when the film

ends. The optimistic
        empty screen at the end
                        of life.

Bridging the Memory

Each instant, a shadow
            of the one before. I
                        am the shadow of a shadow

                        I used to be. When I
                        step into the light my shadow

gains strength, my life
            grows longer. When we arm
                        wrestle we lay down

                        our arms. If my arms
                        were a bridge blood could travel

from my heart to yours, pausing
            midway to admire the distance. Midway
                        to the cemetery I stop for flowers.

                        The vendor's smile
                        is distant. The mountain's

shadow lingers where
            the mountain used to be. Our
                        arms are bridges tired from carrying

                        each other. I
                        wonder: would you mind

if instead of flowers I
            bring the distance to your
                        resting spot.

René Magritte

Snow on the lips, a helmet
          with a hole full of dead ends.

Shadow at the door. This
                    is how we remember the fallen.

Spend your life listening: few
                         answers exist. This is how we fall,

unfinished. This is not
                    an ending.

First

Reciprocation in advance, a simple
rule to combat the world's pre-

carious tilting, its drastic
split into those with

a future and those
without. A gift

given
first.

Blood Exercise

I want to swim in your blood, be
infected by its aliments. I'll

clean up after myself. I won't
tell anyone what we did. Just

leave the vein open. I'll
be there.

Afteretiquette

The house looms before me,
roof trapped   in fog. The many
rooms harbor dead
friends   whose dear faces   have
almost   faded.   Now
I know what the   siren
meant,   angel in   white
beating
my chest,
another
kissing
my
lips,
the silence
after. But how

dare I enter and   meet these
friends   again? Will they   receive
me? They   have waited too
long. Their   ears are   too
small   for words.
And what   have I
done for   them since
they left? Their   gardens
overgrow, their
legacies
lag. I'll
wait   outside
until my   own life's
results
are obsolete.

Hunger for Information

tell me another story
in that language
I don't know

may the syllables
become building blocks
for a lighter life

may vowels sing
all answers
may consonants keep a steady

rhythm of truth
may your story remain
untranslatable

may it be
endless

Round Trip

1

You took a train. I took a train. How could
we know where the rails might
bring us? I dreamed I'd reach you in
my lifetime.

2

Years passed. I had a desk, a chair
in my train car. I didn't leave
the train. Did the train
leave the station?

3

Out the train window, the house
passed like a dream, yet you
knew: inside those blue walls
you had impossibly lived all

these years—your true self, just miles
away. Should you go back? Your small
room: a desk, a chair, the brown
carpet on the stairs. The fields, a still

life through dirty glass. Your fear
of darkness. And in the evening,
into the fields, up the hill, down
the road, to watch the train.

4

The train stopped still like death, and through
the open window, endless fields invaded, wrapped
me in. Red barn, lit up with colors, beckoned,
With years, I found a smaller barn inside,

with a small railroad. And through the small
open window, endless fields.

5

You imagined everything combined, unthinkably
close: my chair, your childhood, my barn, your
fear of darkness, endless fields. Years
passed. I waited for the train whistle. It

never came. I was thinking of you.

6

The train station once existed, and even if
we arrived free of promise, promise
was given us. Even if our times didn't
match, the place did. The rails were removed while

we lingered. The walls crumbled. The empty treads
reminded us of our reasons. And we
reminded each other about each other. If we
invented the train long ago, we can

invent it again, imagine a new life, ride
away together on bright new rails.

7

Years passed. When two trains collided, you
and I landed on a soft patch of grass, no more
hurt than others our age. I shared my thoughts
about how this might end. You frowned, *Why*

should it end?

To Paul Celan

words
stolen
by damaged mouths
spit out
        back to you
with blood on pale skin

you tried to wash them off
        reteach them their meanings
but your slaughtered parents
whispered in your dreams

there comes a time
when no is lighter
than yes
let me visit you a moment before
you go to sleep in the water

to tell you:

of all the words
those you touched became true

of all the almonds
you are the most bitter
        and the sweetest

The Sum of Your Life

Down the street, at the edge of things you know, lie
possibilities you won't explore, loves unused, friendships

unstarted, invitations failed. In the golden light,
years pass, with ghosts of would-be lives

superimposed on would-be paths,
like colored filters. What you are and what

you aspire to, what you've done or tried, all the love
you longed to share with someone who

didn't notice. That day that could have blossomed,
but you were late. What didn't happen is

a part of you.

Appointment with Inner Self

At the center of thought, a small
fading light wrapped in this

wall of body. Who are you, rendered
so slowly out of myself? The river

carries its own bones, holds nothing
longer than its length. The bones

sing their song, blood caresses my veins. I
want to find that place that doesn't

know itself where you and I meet after
this brief engagement. Even if

I'm a lifetime late, I'll
meet you there.

A Study in Luminosity

So long, so without
end, and wouldn't
want one. Your palm

open to seven winds, you ask, *What*
if I stay here until a hill

grows over me, with a river
by its side, a selfish
view, and no memory

of me? I say, *if you were*
the river, I'd be the sky, or

something more solid, to pin
my memory to yours. You rest
your palm on my head, pushing

off as I anchor you. You notice
every living crevice, look into

faces. *Tell me the brightest*
thing. What can I
say? *You*

are the
brightest thing.

100

Ten Questions

How does my memory un
-cover me?

What if I misuse
my eyes?

Are autumn trees happy
to undress?

Can I make up more
than everything?

What will
storm clouds
think
of me?

How do I move
with my love
caught in concrete?

What gift is this
short drive, rusty
engine of us?

When silence
comes, how will I
know to let it in?

How do I sing with all
this past
in my lungs?

Ten Mysteries

1

The team ponder: was a murder committed? The alleged criminal surrenders, yet her confession fails confirmation. Every detail, invented, especially the violence against mannequins. *I remember every moment. I want more of every moment.* History of past crime inconclusive, no crime intentionality observed.

2

The space under the floorboards is recognized as the most likely hiding place. Listening to darkness has this effect. Many years pass.

3

The old woman has been dead all along, even her bones have not been recovered. The suspect is dead. Few clues exist, new ones are welcome. *When memory moves in, reason is amiss, adrift. Give me something else, not what I ask for.* All hidden places will be considered. The aging detective awaits the end of his days wondering what leads to follow in the afterlife.

4

A mannequin's head is found on the pillow. Some experts suggest its baldness is an oblique reference to a hairdresser. *I will not lie to you inside this imagining.* Ominous individuals are involved. Many years pass.

5

Nothing transpires without a series of immeasurably subtle, potentially fateful steps. *Always time, dust. I shiver at the thought of feeling.* Parents shed tears, children shed parents. The body in the broom closet insists that the mystery's façade be examined. No one has turned oneself in. The team debate historical and philosophical texts to take into account.

6

Ominous individuals convince the alleged criminal to sell his body parts. Surveillance equipment is off during key scenes. The hairdresser may be responsible. It's unfair; some of the team cry. *I long to return to the rest of my life and know the road is lost.* Mannequin trafficking is suspected. Many years pass.

7

The mannequin's head shines with its own mental electricity. *I watch you, hear you, feel you inside this envisioning.* Now the old woman is enlisted to travel the world of the dead. She cries herself to sleep every night.

8

Someone has found the money. The upscale residents are adamant the mystery be solved ASAP. *If only I could stay here, inside this listening.* The team are resentful, may sabotage the investigation for the fear that solving the mystery is not in the best interests of all. Many years pass.

9

The old woman wakes to an optimistic sun and scattered commas of clouds. No mail today. *I lose a part of myself in you so I must return to be whole again.* The money is hidden under the floor boards. Everyone she loves is dead. She holds the mannequin in her arms.

10

I want more of every moment after it's happened. Whoever you are, I will not betray you in this remembering.

Ten Fears

Fear of a terrorist
attack during a ten
-car crash

                               Romantic love

           touch me I'm who
             you think I am

Fear of internet
connection loss

                               Love of nature

Fear of personality
theft

                              Love of humanity

       don't touch me I'm who
          you think you are
          or were last time

Fear of earth
-quake

                               Family love

Fear of past
/future self

                            Love of violence

      touch me like the skin
          of a memory
          you love

Your new
private fear

                            Love of science

Fear of pacemaker
removal before
international flights

                            Love of mystery

don't touch me I'm who

I think I am

and fear

Fear of jumping
from a burning
skyscraper

Love of meaning

Fear of un
-popularity

touch me like a dream

or a hope or the best

self

Your own private love

Fear of
drones

Ten Mini-Philosophies

1

If I share something, do you promise not to tell anyone?
Mini-philosophers operate on a limited scale in order
to avoid moral compromises required of their full-
sized counterparts. *You wake up in the morning, you go
outside, you open your umbrella—the leaves keep falling
from the sky, scattered by a generous hand.* A mini-
philosophy is an arbitrary compendium of contrasting
thoughts on a given topic, taken together with their
various interpretations. *You understand: it's autumn,
and there is nothing you can do about it.* Metaphorically
speaking, being a mini-philosopher is a walk in
the park, even if there is no park and one has long
forgotten how to walk. *You keep walking, showered with
bright banners of this late love, letting the cold bottled up
in you mix with the greater cold, with this dank twilight,
with the lazy hiss of the fearful wind.* This sentence is in
a mini-font too small to read.

2

Aristotle is skeptical about differentiating the body
from the mind, but René Descartes argues that the
two are separate. Thomas Henry Huxley thinks of
the conscious mind as a by-product. *If it snows, we
can guess: it's wintertime.* Perhaps sentience itself could
be labeled a side effect of evolution. *And there are no
flowers, only the memory of flowers.* Earlier, panpsychists
think themselves minds among minds. *Doesn't love
exist to bring us joy and pain?* No one has been able to
separate the mind and the body sufficiently to confirm
or deny any hypotheses related to this paradigm. *My*

question is out of place, isn't it? Modern medical science has further blurred the lines, demonstrating that the body may be alive after the brain's death. *Out of place, like all questions.* In this mini-philosophy, the mind serves as the interface for the perceptual interaction with the world, whereas the body is the observer. *In the summertime it snows unwillingly in those mysterious elsewheres you are not privy to.* Metaphorically speaking, some thoughts are exceptionally loud, while others are characterized by the distinct smell of rot. *Who can prove those places still exist?* This sentence is seasoned to perfection and expertly sautéed to excite your palate.

3

This mini-philosophy is your own invention. *You wake up in the morning, you go outside, you open your umbrella: it's snowing. It's wintertime. You are used to hiding under your umbrella, even from the snow.* This sentence waits to be written by you.

4

Plato can be seen as an early defender of women's rights, at a time when most women had very few. *The umbrella becomes heavy, pressed down by the white attracted to the black.* Tullia d'Aragona insists on emotional and romantic freedom for women. *What is the umbrella for?* Simone de Beauvoir affirms that gender affects the perception of personhood and limits one's existentialist perspectives as outlined by Jean-Paul Sartre. *Probably just a habit.* Philosophy's traditional language is comfortable with the convention of "man" in place of "human." *Besides, how could you know the season before you stepped out?* In her philosophical texts Iris Murdoch insists on a moral focus. *After all, windows lie about seasons.* Mini-philosophers investigate the motivations behind the tendency, in many cultural settings, to deny reality to the Other's view of self and the world. *What is better—joy, or pain? you ask yourself.* Metaphorically speaking, this is a lizard's attitude. *This question is also out of place.* Many people are lizards. It has absolutely no relevance to the seasons. Martin Buber and Emmanuel Levinas operate in thinking defined by the Other vs. Descartes' self-centered *cogito ergo sum* and argue that one exists in interaction. *The leaves suspended in the air have no answers.* Maggie Nelson illustrates the challenges that arise from gender (mis)perceptions and the no longer acceptable reduction of gender to its binary Eurocentric meaning. *Perhaps it is you who is incapable of reading the answers on the surface of these leaves—a dried surface tired of life.* This sentence is any gender you like.

5

Wait a minute, there is spring too, isn't there? Plato defines knowledge in terms of belief, but Edmund Gettier digs a hole under this approach, demanding that more stringent criteria be used in verifying knowledge. *We forgot about spring.* Jacob Klein takes Gettier's challenge to heart, arguing that knowledge is essentially impossible without some intuition mixed in. *Why? Because it's autumn, with its panoply of leaves desperately trying to cover this freezing ground?* In this mini-philosophy we pose that knowledge is the ongoing, bi-directional interaction between the subject and the environment. *Or is it because the earth is wearing another one of its masks—the white mask of snow?* Humans are equipped with the capacity to consume a generic field of information concerning the objects in their vicinity and to modify it according to their personal, unique filters for knowledge-perception, which is akin to intuitive reinterpreting of neutral data into data personally felt. *Or simply because it is summertime, and in summer it's silly to dream about the next spring?* The hidden meaning of this sentence remains unexplored.

6

David Hume poses that the self is an illusion. *You wake up in the morning, you go outside.* Saul Smilansky suggests that free will is a necessary illusion. For Bruce Waller, free will and determinism are not mutually exclusive. Adi Shankara insists that Brahman is immune to illusion. *You don't know what you expect to see.* Illusion insists that it is immune to our attempts to constrain the world too tightly. Since our access to empirical data is obtained through the channels of perception and/or intuition, the lovers of trees falling in the forest mention that no statement can be proven or disproven in the absence of the observer. Quantum mechanics contributes that the observer directly impacts the observed. *It's all the same.* In this mini-philosophy, we remove the distinction between the observer and the observed. *Snowdrifts inviting to share in their cool oblivion, colorful pyramids of dry* leaves, flowers with their fragile offer. Metaphorically speaking, we look into the microscope prepared to be examined by the blood sample. *What if we were to mix it all together: the leaves, the snow, the flowers?* We occupy particular spaces in the perceptions of other objects and entities, as well as in their illusions. *But is it worth it?* Metaphorically speaking, we can be the fading memory of a mountain in Japan, or the dream of a penny snug against other pennies in the local cash register. *Does it really make any difference?* We may not even exist at all, neither in the so-called reality, nor in any object's perception. We walk, immaterial until the bitter end, but it may not be bitter, nor an end. As you read this sentence, it makes its own conclusions about you.

7

Remember, you promised not to tell anyone. Bertrand Russell is considerate with the language employed to discuss entities that don't exist. *You can tell now—it doesn't matter anymore.* To Ferdinand de Saussure, language relies on collectivity. *Your promise is what matters.* Jacques Derrida insists on its individuality. *You ask yourself about the meaning of promises, but you know it's a silly question.* To Edward Sapir and Benjamin Whorf, language precedes thought. *The snow is on again.* Vagueness is the aspect of language many thinkers have struggled with and many non-thinkers produced. *It chases you so skillfully: no matter where you hide, it's already there, just as cold and just as white as ever. It's just snow.* Before delving into the topic of language, mini-philosophers prefer to identify which language is being used and to what purpose. *Just frozen water.*

Nothing to be afraid of. Ludwig Wittgenstein demands clarity in our use of language. *Calm down—and it'll melt.* This sentence is in a language unknown to you.

8

The morning comes, and you say goodbye to the moon, and in the evening you say goodnight to the sun. To physicalists, facts determine all other matters. *You go outside, you open your umbrella.* David Chalmers employs philosophical zombies to prove physicalists wrong. *You don't know where you're headed. You've tried everything.* Do brain-dead individuals automatically become philosophical zombies? *Snow is just snow, and even flowers are just flowers.* Even on this, opinions vary. *Not so long ago—last summer—you saw them grow. Maybe it's still summer?* This zombie sentence will devour you through your eyes.

9

Henri Bergson's experience is a mix, a flux of the past and the present, broken into discrete moments for our consumption. *The leaves insist on falling, and you can't believe the trees could have carried so many.* Special relativity concludes that past and present are not absolute. Metaphorically speaking, your past is someone else's future. This is also a literal truth. Marcel Proust compresses all of the protagonist's life into a short list of scenes, each infused with a web of memories and related occurrences. Eternalists agree that time is a vast collection of occurrences that already exist. These attitudes appear to support determinism and strike a blow against free will. When I address you in this account, does the event happen at the moment of my writing or your reading—or is it, in fact, suspended between the two moments? *You promise yourself not to ask unnecessary questions anymore.* In this mini-philosophy, we remove the reliance on the temporal scale in evaluating the emotional and conceptual connections that arise in the modern, highly technological world which demands a reinterpretation of notions such as meaning of life and identity. *Even about love.* Soon we will be our permanent videos, online notes, glimpses of thought. As you read this sentence, I prepare to type these last words.

10

The problem of moral luck references the fact that some individuals find themselves in a more privileged position than many others currently living on Earth. *You wake up in the morning, as usual; you go outside, as usual.* They have more access to necessities and even luxuries. *But the street is gone. And the seasons are gone. There are only the snow, the leaves, the flowers—and soft pink light warming up the world.* With so few needs, they are unlikely to commit crimes of despair such as theft, robbery, and many others. However, it could be argued that the rich are the ones who commit most crimes as they attempt to mold the reality to their needs. *And already it feels as though everything is okay, or almost okay; you have nearly run out of questions: some have been answered, others fell off on their own, like used petals.* Despite the demands of mini-philosophy, you and I inhabit the moral spaces we create for ourselves. *You go outside, transparent and almost invincible. You keep walking until you realize that you are already there.* This sentence believes in you, stranger.

Ten Tools

drone

brain

silence

hand

wheelbarrow

open space

skin

your tool

nuclear bomb

fire

not so much

the open space

but the space

between open things

not so much

the silence

but the knowledge

of after

these
are

my bones in
no
particular order

Ten Love Stories

1

You were the brightest apple, most fit for my hand. My hand was unfit for more. I was seduced by the skin of the brightest apple that fit my eye: broken, fading, then remembered.

2

You stood between the mirror and the tree, the apple in your palm reflectionless. We shared the rules. I entered you, expecting to emerge improved. Inside, a bed, stained mattress, needles, a rusty apple core. A door without a handle, locked behind me. I'm stuck inside your wrong self. Am I the wrong I? They are my needles, my stains, my apple.

3

I paid for apples, you filled my hands with rocks. My train was leaving. Any story is unlikely, and if my story lacked you, apples would fall through my hands. Rocks would fill my dreams. If I don't find you, nothing will ever reach me, not even the moon.

4

Apples, apple trees, apple truths, apple blossoms, lips full of empty promises before the war. How are we to know what remains after years burn? Leaves turned to ashes. Shadow where the tree stood.

5

Who could have known the apple would fall into my
heart, rip me open? Who knew the body was already
ripe? When we fell apart in love and time stopped, the
mystery was laid open. As if we had to bite into our-
selves to know. As if we never were the same.

6

The worm drills the apple as brown rot spreads
through your wellbeing. You find the stars misaligned,
the well in the back yard filled with sand. Some ani-
mals depart, others decay. You write a love letter you'll
never send. My train leaves.

7

The air, the animal, the run, the missing apple, miss-
ing story, missing face. The herebefore with its own
hereafter tailored to our methods of love and ways
of longing. The ends and the promises, and a stained
mattress on a broken bed where no one sleeps. You,
lost elsewhere.

8

You send a letter meant for everyone, like an open
hand or a love song written in ruins, the background
of your life. Your quick moves, efficient body, quick
death. I place an apple on your coffin. I'm still here.

9

When the basket broke, the apples scattered, and no one, not even you, could pick up each one. What we think is love escapes, replaced by a new concept of love to fit the new self. You enter me. The apples disappear.

10

I was a simple apple. My train was leaving. You picked me up, laid me in your basket. I lie, chosen.

Ten Silences

for John Cage

1

2

3

4

5

6

7

8

9

10

Ten Theories

1

The street ends in a dead end, a space removed. Air currents flow around it. **Fading gravity.** You, inside, at least in theory. *It takes a lot of bulbs to light the world.*

2

I arrived before too early. I remember your birthmark. *Now it's no longer too late.* **Symptoms reemerge.** They all agree: you grow daily.

3

A dry leaf on my porch makes more noise than a jackhammer. **I blame myself.** You are exemplary, like the brightest of recent stars. I won't disclose my unimportant identity.

4

My mind a kaleidoscope. Matter emerges into being: grass blades from granite, muscled fingers at the ends of iron bars, each fence shivering with finger-twisting. **As if there ever were another way.** *So many lives to revisit as the leaf descends.*

5

You've never understood why air is so attracted to you, its molecules insistent like children. They never seem to leave you alone. **My empty space where you were.** *I'm still trying to answer that question you asked years ago.*

6

When I burn out, who will replace me? You are more in-tended than real. They all agree: you are a puzzle. **You grow in my memory.** You are here.

7

You are particular, subatomic, defined by contrast, steeped in absence. *You mentioned fireflies.* They all agree: your eyes are brighter than the space around them, each iris a path into a distinct afterlife. **Did you really mean it that way?** I remember that birthmark shaped like a question on your shoulder.

8

I turn the steering wheel 360 degrees. You defy gravity, you defy the lack of gravity. *Now I understand a straight line.* **I will lie to you often in this account.** We hold concepts in our hands like rusty weapons as our children gather dust.

9

You are not what some think you are, nor what I imagine. *When my life was empty, I planted question marks along my path.* **I wish you noticed.** Centuries smile at my attempts to summarize you. *Now that leaves have arrived, I can't remember my questions.* At a lost street crossing, you wait for yourself.

10

You move, quintessential, unlike most of us. You let the street go where it wants. The missing space floats, a memory in its own right. *A bulb in the ground turns into light on its own terms.* **I open the window so I may see you, some day.** Your eyes are brighter than mine. The birthmark on your shoulder. They all agree: you grow out of everything while I creep in cracks between better things.

Ten Tens

Ten

victories imagined
like a city

of smoke, ten

grinning fires, ten
rivers trying

to escape, ten

friends wrapped
in their sad

endings, ten

mysteries unsolved,
one

merge lane for ten

hopes guiding
our lives, ten

fears that formed us, ten

errors of love, ten
reasons we pass

like rain, ten

ways we last in each
other.

Ten Doors

Don't go back to sleep. —Rumi

1

Windows open, eyes close. Nothing disturbs the dust on the road. Today, the bombs fall elsewhere.

2

A traveler returns to her hometown after years abroad. Is this really her hometown? *Whatever else may happen, I want to share this memory.* The traveler walks the streets, stares inquisitively. Only you can help her. You live here. No one else is aware of her arrival. You put down your book and welcome her at the door.

3

Your lips are a broken door. Unencumbered by solidity, I flow out the water tap, slide past your fingers, wish away the beauty of your wound, a wound I inflicted before regretting it.

4

You ring, not expecting anyone to open. When the door budges, you are unsurprised to find no one behind it. You explore the multitude of empty rooms. You are the host. You've lived here all your life. *I will not lie to you inside this imagining.* You will die here one day. Any day is one day. You hear the bell.

5

When the bombing stops, I hope the quiet will remain. You may still exist as a whole – a single being built from compliant atoms. Without a warning, my eyes close. *I watch you, hear you, feel you inside this refocusing.* Random fire wakes me. Come in quietly, so I believe you are real. The door is open. I am not asleep.

6

Instruments of light left at the door. *You hear the bell.*

7

You long for some breaking and entering. The door is just a point of view. The way here no longer exists. *You and I are alone in this envisioning.* You are the host. You stretch the corners of your lips with your index fingers until a matching smile emerges in the mirror. Not every door is locked.

8

I'm mesmerized by your contours. Close the door. *I slide past your fingers.* The land is out of sight on a frozen map. *If only I could be silent here, inside this listening.* We trace our own steps on a vast green sheet covered with snow.

9

When you touch, I touch. Maybe this is not enough. *When do we begin if not a lifetime back?* The bombing continues. We run away from ourselves. This is not my hometown. *These are not my thoughts.* Please open the door. These are not my bombs, not my memory.

10

Any town is hometown. I am not asleep. *Whoever you are, I want to be with you inside this remembering.*

About the Author

A. Molotkov's previous poetry collections are *The Catalog of Broken Things*, *Application of Shadows*, and *Synonyms for Silence*. His memoir *A Broken Russia Inside Me* (Propertius) deals with growing up in the USSR and making a new life in America. Molotkov's collection of ten short stories, *Interventions in Blood*, is part of *Hawai'i Review* Issue 91. He co-edits *The Inflectionist Review*, and his past work includes visual art, experimental film and music. He plays percussion and the Armenian duduk. Please visit him at AMolotkov.com.

About The Word Works

Since its founding in 1974, The Word Works has published volumes of contemporary poetry and presented public programs. Its imprints include The Washington Prize, The Tenth Gate Prize, The Hilary Tham Capital Collection, and International Editions. Monthly, The Word Works offers free literary programs in its Café Muse and Poets vs The Pandemic series, and each summer it holds free poetry programs in its Joaquin Miller Poetry Series which also presents two high school winners of the Jacklyn Potter Young Poets Competition. As a 501(c)3 organization, The Word Works has received awards from the National Endowment for the Arts, the National Endowment for the Humanities, the D.C. Commission on the Arts & Humanities, the Witter Bynner Foundation, Poets & Writers, The Writer's Center, Bell Atlantic, the David G. Taft Foundation, and others, including many generous private patrons. The Word Works is a member of the Community of Literary Magazines and Presses and its books are distributed by Small Press Distribution.

❧ wordworksbooks.org ❧

Other Word Works Books

Annik Adey-Babinski, *Okay Cool No Smoking Love Pony*
Karren L. Alenier, *Wandering on the Outside*
      From the Belly: Appreciating Tender Buttons V. I (ed.)
Jennifer Barber, *The Sliding Boat Our Bodies Made*
Andrea Carter Brown, *September 12*
Christopher Bursk, ed., *Cool Fire*
Willa Carroll, *Nerve Chorus*
Grace Cavalieri, *Creature Comforts*
      The Long Game: New & Selected Poems
Abby Chew, *A Bear Approaches from the Sky*
Nadia Colburn, *The High Shelf*
Henry Crawford, *Binary Planet*
Barbara Goldberg, *Berta Broadfoot and Pepin the Short*
Akua Lezli Hope, *Them Gone*
Frannie Lindsay, *If Mercy*
Elaine Magarrell, *The Madness of Chefs*
Chloe Martinez, *Ten Thousand Selves*
Marilyn McCabe, *Glass Factory*
      Don't Get Me Started
JoAnne McFarland, *Identifying the Body*
Leslie McGrath, *Feminists Are Passing from Our Lives*
Kevin McLellan, *Ornitheology*
A. Molotkov, *Future Symptoms*
Ann Pelletier, *Letter That Never*
W.T. Pfefferle, *My Coolest Shirt*
Ayaz Pirani, *Happy You Are Here*
Robert Sargent, *Aspects of a Southern Story*
      A Woman from Memphis
Roger Smith, *Radiation Machine Gun Funk*
Julia Story, *Spinster for Hire*
Cheryl Clark Vermeulen, *They Can Take It Out*
Julie Marie Wade, *Skirted*
Miles Waggener, *Superstition Freeway*
Fritz Ward, *Tsunami Diorama*
Camille-Yvette Welsh, *The Four Ugliest Children in Christendom*
Amber West, *Hen & God*
Maceo Whitaker, *Narco Farm*
Nancy White, ed., *Word for Word*